T0162086

No part of this publication may be reproduced or transmitted in any form or by any means without the prior permission of the publisher. Any copy of this book issued by the publisher as a paperback or hardback is sold subject to the condition that it shall not by way of trade or otherwise be lent, resold, hired out or otherwise circulated without the publishers' prior consent in any form of binding or cover other than which it is published and without a similar condition including these words being imposed on a subsequent purchaser.

©2016 Pro-actif Communications Ltd

Written by Patrick Potter

A catalogue record for this book is available from the British Library.

First Edition 2016.
First published in Great Britain in 2016 by Carpet Bombing Culture.
An imprint of Pro-actif Communications
www.carpetbombingculture.co.uk
email: books@carpetbombingculture.co.uk
©Carpet Bombing Culture. Pro-actif Communications
ISBN: 978-1-908211-43-9

CARPET
BOMBING
CULTURE

www.carpetbombingculture.co.uk

INTERVIEW
YOU

WHO DO YOU THINK YOU ARE?

WELCOME TO THE WORLD EXCLUSIVE INTERVIEW WITH YOU

In this bumper book of scintillating interrogatives (questions) you can have a blast and rediscover yourself all at the same time. All you have to do is pick a random page and ask yourself a whole bunch of questions.

Simple as that.

But don't stop there! You can use this book just about any way your heart desires. Each page of questions can be directed at just about anybody, anytime, anywhere. The you in Interview You can be any you who you'd like to interview. Clear as crystal, right?

I knew we were on the same wavelength.

Have fun!

THE BOOK WHERE YOU ARE THE STAR

With a little luck, a playful attitude and a dash of honesty you might just learn to fall in love with yourself. It's a mirror made of questions for you to gaze in and ask 'mirror mirror on the wall, who shall I be this lifetime...?'

You are already a superstar to someone.

The rest is just an epic game of angels with dirty faces playing hide and seek with each other till the lights go out.

The bell rings. The round begins.

Every turn needs a new player, and you are all the players rolled into one.

Discover yourself or create yourself?
It means the same thing.
And you don't stop. You can't stop.
Bought the ticket. Taking the ride.

When the time comes to invent, or reinvent yourself - come back to the mirror. Look inside to go outside. Find something inside you that the world needs. Now take it out into the world. And... repeat forever.

Am I ready?

Hell, yeah.

Take the stage...

THE RIGHT QUESTION

One afternoon sat in a bar with the gang from work. We were all chatting away. Everybody at the table was talking about work. We had just spent the whole week together in the office working and yet there we were talking workplace gossip. Did we have to be so predictable?

I mused to my neighbour - did you notice that everybody here is talking about work. With a cruel glint in her eye she raised her voice and got the attention of the whole group, a dozen or so people. 'Hey - this guy has something much more interesting to talk about!'

All eyes were on me. But she had made a fatal error. She had given me an audience.

"Has anyone ever nearly died?" I asked.

A momentary pause. A few quizzical looks. Then one voice piped up. And suddenly the entire table erupted into several passionate discussions about near death experiences. The minutae of the office grind was instantly forgotten.

I flashed a glance back at my neighbour. She conceded defeat with a rueful grin.

Even I was shocked at how effective the question was. I learned something right then. A big thunderclap realisation.

AT THE RIGHT TIME

People are much more interesting than they think they are.

The right question at the right time can break that mask and inspire new developments in our relationships with each other. A series of random questions is even better, a powerful tool for shocking some life back into the art of conversation. Or even just a way to reflect on who you are right now, on every level from the trivial to the deep. (Because nothing is really trivial.)

Why should good questions be reserved for celebrity interviews and public radio shows?

You are not your job. You are not your schoolwork. You are not 'that person'. You are just as complex, nuanced, shifting and fascinating as any so-called icon that ever lived. It is through artful conversation that you can experience this wonderful complexity that you are and enjoy that same complexity in others.

Let's reclaim the conversation. Because it's the most fun you can have with your clothes on.

Do you want to play?

THIS IS A GAME OF SELF-DISCOVERY.

OR IS IT A GAME OF SELF-CREATION?

THE METHOD OF RANDOM

'Interview You' uses the **'Method of Random'** to draw you quickly and deeply into the most fascinating possible conversation with one of the most interesting people in the world today - you! The method is inspired by the art of conversation.

This is what **Interview You** tries to initiate with its semi-random bouquets of questions.

They come at you from several angles at once, like life.

The fun is the unexpected twists and turns that open up space for you to surprise yourself with your own answers.

Interview You is above all, a game. It should be played lightly. The randomness helps to keep you on your toes and encourages you not to overthink your answers.

So think fast. Ask a lot of questions in a short space of time. Read the question - interpret it however you will and start to answer before your internal censors have a chance to review and censor your replies. Just don't edit yourself. This is meant to be a catharsis.

HOW TO
USE THIS BOOK

- Relax and enjoy yourself - it's meant to be fun.

- Unplug and tune out. Switch off your phone. Focus on yourself.

- Take time on your own to answer the questions and do the sections in any order you like.

- You can also play the book party style, taking turns with friends to answer random questions.

- Don't be shy, why not share the love? Use the questions as a gateway to find out more about people around you.

Disclaimer

There are a lot of questions in this book and many of them are silly but some of them are about real life and it is possible that one or two of them may upset you. It is absolutely not our intention to upset anyone - we want this to be a positive ride and we wholeheartedly apologise for any unintentional triggers. Keep on the sunny side. x

YOUR MISSION

Most people don't play for the epic win. Most people play it safe. Everybody says it is the right thing to do. Be sensible. Be realistic. In reality it's often harder to get the things that people think are 'realistic'. Why? Because everybody else is competing with you to get those things.

When you aim unrealistically high there is less competition.

Choose five **TOTALLY UNREALISTIC** goals for your life and write them down on a piece of paper.

The nature of the universe is epic. When you set out to achieve epic things the whole universe conspires to help you achieve them.

Your mission is to raise the level of epicness in the universe.

Do you accept?

Sign here...

LIFE IS BETTER WHEN YOU ASK MORE QUESTIONS

INTERVIEW YOU helps you figure out who you really are by helping you to figure out what you really think. Here are some random applications:

Quality Time

Tumbleweed rolls across the dinner table. You pick up the book, flip it open and read out a dozen questions - no effort, the conversation comes, bringing you all back to life. Boom!

Random Acts of Curiosity

Why not start asking more questions - random questions to random people at random times. Start a micro-revolution. No more alienation. Maybe ask the postman what their favourite movie is. Small steps, right? Maybe ask the waiter the first five questions on the first page. Then get braver. Maybe even ask your parents.

The Couple

How long has it been since those early days? What happened to those long conversations? Hey, do you want to play a game? I'm going ask you twenty questions out of this book. Then we swap over...

Fifteen Minutes of Fame

Why not make all of your friends feel like they're famous? Why not interview them all? Plan it all out. Get them to film you up close. Twenty questions - that way you can show them what kind of thing you want. Then share the clips with your friends. An instant time capsule. Even do your mom too.

Study Break

Any more cramming tonight and it'll feel like your head is going to explode. Ok. You want to feel like a human being! So you and your study buddies break out the snacks and Interview You. Rapid fire round. No hesitation! Parents downstairs wondering how you can have so much fun studying.

Creative Commute

Some nights you wish you could just teleport home. But it's ok. Flip open your book and do a couple of sections. Remind yourself of who you are before you get home. Leave your work self on the train - get off as a human being.

The Reanimator

You know those zombie friendships? They live on, shuffling through your social media accounts long after they died a natural death. Time to get on a mission to reanimate a few. Maybe photograph a page of the book and send it to everyone. Maybe, just maybe that list of random questions can put the spark of life back into a few of them!

Reasons to be cheerful. Part 1

Do you want to be successful? Ask yourself why

Now ask again. Keep asking, like a child, until you get to the deepest reason - the bedrock. Are there wrong reasons and right reasons? Do your reasons change or stay the same? Does it even matter? Are we inspired by our dreams or trapped in them?

Reasons to be successful. Delete as appropriate.

I want to be adored.
I want a life of drama.
I want adventure.
I want it all.
I want a garage full of fancy cars.
I want a palace to live in.
I want the highs
I want the lows
I want to be a hero to somebody.
I want to make all the people I love happy.
I want to be able to provide for everyone in my tribe.
I want to have status and respect.
I want freedom. I want to roam the earth as I please.
I want legacy.
I want a voice. I want to change the world.
I want the power to defend something.
I want the power to destroy something.
I want to use my talents for the good of the community.
I want to live forever.

Everybody wants to be successful. No exceptions.
OK maybe there are a few exceptions, but probably much fewer than you might think.

PART ONE
DISCOVER YOURSELF

Questions that help you figure out who you are and what you want to say to the world.

Let's play a game.

Imagine that you are a superstar.

Now, because you believe it
you act like you believe it,
you talk like you believe it
and you think like you believe it.

Now other people believe it
because you believe it.

Now it's true.

TO BE OR NOT TO BE?

THESE ARE THE QUESTIONS...

ATOMIC ICEBREAKERS #1

There are many ways to break the ice, but perhaps the best way is with a hydrogen bomb. That'll break just about any piece of ice you can mention. If the room is still a little frosty, try the greenhouse effect. Always gets the ice melting. But seriously. I'm here all week.

1. What are you wearing right now?

2. Where did you get it?

3. How much is your whole outfit worth?

4. Which is your favourite cheese?

5. Have you ever nearly died?

6. What is your party trick?

7. Can you describe the way that you dance in one word?

8. Do you make things?

9. What is the first thing that comes into your head right now?

10. Are there any of the cheeses which you do not care for?

11. Who is your celebrity crush?

12. What are you really bad at?

13. How much is a litre of milk?

X OR Y?

If you absolutely positively definitely had to choose between the two following things – which would you choose. You can't say both or neither. You have to choose one. Well, you can do whatever you want really but it's more fun if you play by the rules. Rules or cheating?

Cats or Dogs?

Sitcom or Documentary?

Books or TV?

Tea or Coffee?

Go Invisible or Be Able to Fly?

Night Owl or Early Bird?

Sporty or Arty?

Call or Text?

Romantic or Realistic?

Rock or Hip Hop?

Digital or Analogue?

Retro or Contemporary?

America or Europe?

Asia or Africa?

Fairies or Unicorns?

Apple or Android?

Thrift Store or Flagship Store?

ATOMIC
ICEBREAKERS #2

It's always good to start with the small talk. Soften them up before you drop the big one. Lovely weather we're having today! What happens when we die? BOOM! Now we're finally talking.

1. On a scale of 1-10 how much do you love eating?

2. If we came to your house, what would you cook for us, if anything

3. Do you enjoy being the centre of attention or flying under the radar?

4. What's your favourite children's TV programme from when you were little.

5. What posters did you have on your bedroom wall at the age of twelve?

6. Who was your best friend at school?

7. Do you have any guilty pleasures?

8. How should one ideally cook a butternut squash?

9. What can money not buy?

10. What's your favourite ice cream flavour?

11. Which book would you like to read again?

12. What are you looking forward to?

SNAPPY CHAT #1

Welcome to Mastermind.
Your specialist subject is: 'random'. Go!

Think fast! Shoot from the lip. Set a timer on your phone. 2 minutes. 14 questions. Unedited, live and uncensored. No preparation and no cheating! Say the first thing that comes into your head. Are you ready to play?

3....2....1....GO!

What is your current word of the moment?

Who is your team?

Give me one word that describes the place where you live?

What was your favourite subject at school?

What is the weirdest thing you've ever eaten?

Who is your favourite solo artist of all time?

Who was your favourite teacher?

Using only one word describe the town you grew up in?

What is the best album of all time?

What is the best single of all time?

What is your current favourite programme on TV?

Who was your least favourite teacher?

Who is your favourite band of all time?

If you could sing a duet with any person living or dead, who would it be?

DIGGING DEEP

So I feel like we are developing a bond of trust here. And maybe it's time to get a little deeper. Maybe we can afford to take a few more conversational risks. Open up a little more. What do you say?

1. What's the biggest thing on your mind right now?

2. Which motivates you more, failure or success?

3. Who or what makes you angry?

4. What's the hardest thing you have to cope with right now?

5. What one thing have you been putting off doing?

6. If you could give your younger self one piece of advice, what would it be?

7. What headline would you like to read in tomorrow's newspaper?

8. Does god exist?

9. What is your biggest regret?

10. Would you steal to feed your family?

11. Would you kill to protect your family?

12. You bump another car while leaving the car park and nobody saw you do it, do you leave your name and address on their windscreen?

WHO ARE YOU?

AGREE TO DISAGREE

Answer true or false to the following statements:

1. Beauty is in the eye of the beholder.

2. There is no such thing as luck.

3. An unanalysed life is not worth living.

4. People mostly get what they deserve.

5. If you are positive on the inside you attract positive energy.

6. If someone bullies you, hit them back harder.

7. You get more with honey than vinegar.

8. People will take advantage if you show weakness.

9. You have to share your vulnerability to build trust.

10. Spare the rod, spoil the child.

11. Ignorance is bliss.

12. The things that you own end up owning you.

13. A bird in the hand is worth two in the bush.

14. Guns don't kill people; people kill people.

EVERYBODY GET RANDOM #1

If you always do what you've always done you'll always get what you've always got.

1. Have you had your fifteen minutes of fame?

2. How do you feel about zoos?

3. Have you ever had to be brave?

4. What is a perfect day for you?

5. What do you want written on your gravestone?

6. Have you got rhythm?

7. Can you spell rhythm?

8. Can you whistle?

9. What do you want for your Birthday?

10. How weak are you?

11. Who would you like to punch in the face?

12. Is Big Brother watching you?

13. Do your bathroom scales lie to you?

14. Do you ever think about making preparations for the apocalypse?

ASK A STOOPID QUESTION

The most dangerous of all the monkeys is the one who thinks he isn't dumb.

1. How long could you survive without any money?

2. What is your Thanksgiving dish?

3. What is your purpose on this earth?

4. Which carnivore are you?

5. What songs can you remember all the lyrics to?

6. What song can you not remember the title of?

7. What is your spirit animal?

8. What would happen to you in the Hunger Games?

9. If you were a soap opera character how would you be killed off?

10. Which superhero comic character are you?

11. Which Disney character are you?

12. Which country should you live in?

13. Which city should you live in?

FAME IS GIVING PEOPLE

WHO

DON'T KNOW WHAT THEY

WANT

SOMETHING TO WANT.

DIGGING DEEPER

Yep you guessed it, this might get uncomfortable.

1. What makes you angry?

2. Would you sacrifice your own life to save the life of 100 strangers?

3. What frightens you?

4. What do you not mind spending a lot of money on?

5. If you could say one thing to your 50 year old self what would it be?

6. If you could say one thing to your 15 year old self what would it be?

7. Does power corrupt?

8. Are we alone in the universe?

9. You find some cash on the floor while waiting in the queue. Do you ask the people around you to see if anyone has dropped it?

10. Is kissing cheating?

11. If you discovered your best friend had committed a crime and the police were appealing for information would you report them?

12. Would you rather know the date of your death or the cause of your death?

13. What do you give and who do you give it to?

GET OFF
THE FENCE!

In polite company it is considered wise not to commit to a divisive opinion on anything too heavy. Well, you're not in polite company now. There may be two sides to every story – but in the court of judgement you have to choose one.

Now get down off that fence before you fall off!

Evolution
Fact or Fiction?

Digital Piracy
Empowering the People or Robbing the Artists?

Edward Snowden
Hero or Traitor?

Meat
Immoral Addiction or Vital Nutrition?

Prison
Offender Rehabilitation or Flat Out Punishment?

Fracking
Great Source of Energy or A High Pressure Injection of Poison Directly into the Water Table?
(OK this one is a leading question LOL)

Assisted Suicide
Mercy Killing or Legalised Murder?

GET OFF
THE FENCE!

Legalise Drugs
Sound Strategy or Misguided Liberalism?

Right to Bear Arms
Fundamental Freedom or Mental Aberration?

War on Terror
CIA Conspiracy or Genuine Threat?

Kanye West
The Greatest Artist of the Last Three Generations
or A Monomaniac?

Minimum Wage
Social Progress or Attack on Small Business?

Immigration
Healthy or Dangerous?

Gay Marriage
Yes or No?

Donald Trump
Man of the People or Insane Demagogue?

Climate Change
Fact or Fiction?

Capital Punishment
Dead Wrong or Hang 'em High

You are the unreliable narrator

They say you never step in the same river twice. Every time you step into it, it's always already a different river. Every time you tell the story of yourself you tell it from a different perspective.

It ain't like there is no such thing as truth. Just maybe that the closest we can ever get to it is farther away than most people think. We are, bless us, self-serving monkeys, and we can't help but use the past always in a partisan way - as a tool to help us reinforce and authenticate whoever it is we are pretending to be in this present moment.

We edit our personal history. Always have. Trouble is now, it gets more difficult when there is so much digital evidence out there. No matter. You can always add a little spin.

If you are interested in the truth, and you want to chase after it, like a dog chasing it's own tail, then you could do worse than this. Try asking yourself the questions in this book as if you were not you, as if you were some faceless-eternal-alien-entity, some kind of inhuman observer. Now that's a parlour game that could get out of hand.

Can you see through your own bull? Can you catch a glimpse of the you that other people experience? Can you feel your effect on the world without bias?

Maybe the greatest illusion, the one that permits us to believe in selfhood, is the illusion of continuity. You are not the baby in those baby pictures.

Is there really an essential, unchanging 'you' or are you more like a river?

They say you never ask the same person a question twice...

EVERYBODY GET RANDOM #2

Let the chips fall where they lay and the devil take the hindmost. Onward!

1. Do you have any special skills?

2. How often do you sing?

3. Will you sing a little bit right now?

4. What do you do when you can't sleep?

5. What is the luckiest thing you have ever found?

6. The most beautiful place you have ever seen?

7. What games are you playing these days?

8. What are you into right now?

9. Can you change a car tyre?

10. What are you finding ANNOYING in this great charade we call modern life?

11. If you were the next President of the United States, what would you go to work on first?

12. How do you feel when you hear your national anthem?

13. Do you remember life before the internet?

TELL ME SOMETHING YOU'VE NEVER TOLD ANYONE ELSE?

THE DREAMER'S DISEASE

As a wise man once said. Wake up kid. Anyone can dream big. What have you done today to bring you closer to your dreams? And that does not include taking a nap in the lunch hour.

1. Who are the most influential people in your life?

2. What do you spend the most money on?

3. Do you sing in the shower?

4. Can you describe yourself in three words?

5. What would you rather be doing right now?

6. What actions are you taking to realise your dreams?

7. What are you looking forward to most, today?

8. What are you looking forward to most, this week?

9. What are you looking forward to most, this year?

10. OK, imagine you're a TV chat show host and you get to pick the interviewees for Saturday's prime time show, which three guests do you pick?

11. What would the show be called?

12. Who would the house band be?

LET'S PLAY
AT BEING
RICH AND FAMOUS.

IT'S PROBABLY
MORE FUN
THAN BEING
RICH AND FAMOUS.

NO TIME TO WASTE

If it isn't on your 'to do' list then it is a waste of time. Or is it a waste of time to make a 'to do' list? You could write your 'to do' list at the end of the day - then everything you do will be retroactively validated as a completed task. Genius. Thank me later.

1. If you .... by the end of the day it'll be an epic win.

2. If you .... by the end of the year it'll be a glorious victory.

3. If you .... within five years it'll be a legendary triumph.

4. When you leave your mark on the world it will be ....

5. If you can just .... then you'll be ready to die happy.

6. If you could change just one thing in your past then what would it be?

7. Who in your life made you feel like you couldn't be a star?

8. Who always made you feel you were a star?

9. What is your most likeable quality?

10. If you could ask anyone in the world one question, who and what would you ask?

11. Tell me one thing that is on your bucket list?

SNAPPY CHAT #2

> Welcome to snappy chat. It's like a chat but snappier.

2 minutes. 20 questions.
3....2....1....GO!

What's the best theatre production you've seen?

Which movie made you cry?

What's your favourite movie in the last 12 months?

What's the last album you listened to?

What's the last album you bought?

Who's your favourite DJ of all time?

If you had a boat what would you call it?

Three little things that make you smile?

What is your most treasured possession?

What is your smallest bad habit?

What is your biggest vice?

When was the last time you cried?

What movie would you like to see a sequel to?

What's your favourite junk food?

Something you used to like but don't anymore?

What's your favourite sport?

What's the last song you listened to?

Would you rather be fluent in all languages or be able to play every musical instrument?

What was the name of your first pet?

How would you describe yourself in one word?

MY PAD

Your latest project just blew up and you have become a bona fide superstar. As the money starts flooding in you realise that it's finally time to buy that epic dream home. You get together an elite team of real estate agents, interior designers and architects and design your new crib.

When the MTV Cribs film crew come knocking at your door - what will we see...

1. Where is your crib?

2. Who lives in it?

3. What is the style?

4. Talk us through three of your favourite rooms.

5. Tell us about your favourite eccentric features.

6. Do you have a basketball court, cinema, den, games room, boat dock, tennis court, fire pit, sauna, spa, hot tub or swimming pool? Or all of them?

7. What's in the garage?

8. What art do you have on the walls?

Famous people are boring. This book is a billion times more interesting than any interview with any famous person ever. **How is that so?** Superstars have so much interesting stuff going on in their lives. They are always in new places, wearing new clothes, working on new projects, sleeping with new people. Surely they are the most interesting people on Earth? Meh. Not as interesting as you. Seriously.

Why is that? Because you are not a brand. You don't have to be afraid of being inconsistent. You don't live for the sake of an audience.

They are never going to tell the truth, not even to themselves. You have nothing to lose. No teleprompter, no script, no rehearsal. Real people are much more interesting than celebs.

You are a Real Person.

And like all real things you are a mess of light and shade, an ever changing complexity, an oil slick and a rainbow - ambiguous, neither right nor wrong - a glorious collection of imperfections.

IMAGINARY SITUATIONS #1

LOST IN SPACE

You have been selected to lead a manned mission to the farthest reaches of the galaxy. You will be trapped for decades in a tin box floating light years away from home. If you survive you'll be cryogenically frozen only to be reanimated on Earth 1000 years from now. Before you leave you must make some mission critical decisions...

1. Choose your crew. Who are the three people you will take with you and why?

2. You can take three personal items with you on the mission. What do you choose and why?

3. How will you spend your last days on Earth?

4. How will you entertain yourself in the vast emptiness of space?

5. What will you say to the people of the future about the times in which you lived your previous life on Earth?

6. How does your story end?

QUESTIONS
can be weapons.

QUESTIONS
can be lies just as easily as answers.

QUESTIONS
are made out of our presumptions about the world.

QUESTIONS
can be wrong just as easily as answers.

GET OFF
THE FENCE!

Celebrity Culture
Banal and Vacuous or Fun and Harmless?

Recycling
Waste of Effort or Every Little Helps?

Big Tech Tax
Tax Avoidance or Tax Evasion?

Cosmetic Surgery
If You Can Afford It Flaunt It or Just Say No?

Graffiti
Art or Vandalism?

Political Lobbying
Snakes in the Grass or Legitimate Advocacy?

Animal Experimentation
Indefensible Mutilation or Indispensable Progress?

Free Press
Troubadors for Truth or Chequebook Journalism?

International Aid
Charity Begins at Home or Feed the World?

Open Borders
Close The Doors We're Full or Come One, Come All?

SNAPPY CHAT #3

> Think of a number between one and 18. Take that question and text it to the person who last texted you. No explanations.

2 minutes. 18 questions.
3....2....1....GO!

Your style in one word is...?

What is your phobia?

What is your spirit animal?

What are you reading right now?

What is your favourite country?

What is your favourite book?

What's your favourite place to hang out?

What is your guilty pleasure?

What is one talent that you wish you had?

What could you not live without?

Who is your icon?

What word do you think is overused?

What do you find overrated?

What is your favourite museum?

What's your secret talent?

Who is your favourite comedian?

If you could spend 24 hours with anyone (living or dead) who would it be?

What would you do together?

ALL T NO SHADE

It isn't throwing shade if it comes from a place of truth, right? Truth hurts. Truth comes from a place of truth. It's called Truth Land. You can take the kids there on holiday. It's great. A word of warning - there is no shade at Truth Land, so you will need sun block. Stay classy.

1. Would you want to be your own friend?

2. Are you the kind of person you would hang out with?

3. What is the meaning of life?

4. Do you know first aid?

5. Could you give someone CPR?

6. Would you rather fail at something epic or succeed at something mundane?

7. Who would you give three wishes to?

8. If you could make anyone in the world your slave for a day who would it be and what would you make them do?

9. If it was easy to switch, would you consider being a different gender for a day?

10. Your house is on fire. There are no people inside. You can save one thing. What do you choose?

11. You have won $1,000,000 Brewster Style and you have to give it all away by midnight. What do you do?

Some questions,
you ask them
a thousand times
and the answer
is always the same.

**WHERE ARE
YOU FROM?**

Some questions
you ask you get
a different
answer every time.

**WHERE ARE
YOU GOING?**

I'M LOSING CONTROL

Uh oh. She's lost control again. Just keep throwing questions at her. She'll come back down from there in her own time. We can tidy up later.

1. How much toast is too much?

2. If you could travel back fifteen minutes and give yourself a quick message what would you say to yourself?

3. What is the first piece of poetry that comes into your head? (Lyrics count)

4. Have you ever been really really hungry?

5. Have you ever been out of control?

6. What invention would you like to see created in the next ten years?

7. You pick up a brass lamp in a thrift store and while cleaning it a genie appears with the "I'll give you three wishes" routine. What do you ask for?

8. Should we struggle to control the beast within or accept our baser nature?

9. How would your friends describe you?

NOTHING BUT MAMMALS

Beneath the illusion of control ancient animal codes drive us like meaty automobiles.

1. Rate your own posture on a scale of one to ten.

2. How much do you know about nutrition?

3. Have you ever (or do you now) take photographs of your meals for the purposes of distributing them on social media?

4. How big is your personal space?

5. Can you touch your toes?

6. Do you ever enter into physical combats?

8. Do you think you could beat a large dog in a fight?

9. What if you had to do it in order to defend someone you love?

10. Are you any good at climbing trees?

11. Are you a product of nature or nurture?

12. On a scale of 1 to 10 how similar are you to your parents, in your beliefs and values?

WE LIVE IN THE FUTURE

You can buy a watch that communicates with your phone and tells you things that your phone was already telling you. That's how much we live in the future. I can't even keep up, can you? You can see stuff in 3D on the TV now! You can also see in 3D in the real world using your eyes. Madness. Maybe one day the machines will collectively realise that humanity is awesome and decide to serve us loyally forever.

1. Are you the same person who first opened this book?

2. Are we alone in the universe?

3. Do you believe in ghosts?

4. Have you had any unexplained experiences?

5. Is there a right and wrong? Or are these concepts flexible?

6. How should we decide what is right and what is wrong?

7. Is it OK for some people to be rich when most people are poor?

SNAPPY CHAT #4

See if you can answer all twenty of these questions while dancing vigorously at the same time. Get your friend to shout the questions at you while you crunk.

2 minutes. 17 questions.

3....2....1....GO!

How many languages can you speak?

What's your IQ?

What language do you wish you could speak?

What's the most beautiful thing in the world?

What scares you the most?

What do you collect?

Would you rather travel back in time or forward to the future?

Are you superstitious?

What is the best album cover design of all time?

Do you prefer painting or photography?

If you could have written any song in history what would it be?

What's the worst album that you own?

Who is the greatest sportsperson of all time?

Who is your favourite visual artist of all time?

What is the greatest work of art ever?

How do you feel in an art gallery?

What makes you go to bed early?

IN ONE WORD

Try this exercise for fun and games. Don't think. Scan down the list of famous people and say the first word that comes into your head. Do it fast. Do it with a friend and compare results. What do your answers say about you?

Tom Cruise	Steven Spielberg
Lance Armstrong	Beyonce
Kanye West	Donald Trump
Kim Kardashian	Stephen Hawking
Taylor Swift	Amy Winehouse
George W. Bush	Martin Scorsese
Oprah Winfrey	Bono
Michael Jackson	Bill Cosby
Queen Elizabeth II	Christopher Nolan
Charlie Sheen	Paris Hilton
Justin Bieber	Barack Obama
Bill Gates	Miley Cyrus
Simon Cowell	Hillary Clinton
Julian Assange	Selena Gomez
Cristiano Ronaldo	Adele
Kim Jong-Un	Gwyneth Paltrow

IF I RULED
THE WORLD...

Absolute power corrupts absolutely. Sounds like a lot of fun, right? What if every dang fool in the world actually jumped when you said jump?

1. What cause are you passionate about?

2. If you could bring one person back from the dead who would it be?

3. If you could change one thing in the world right now, what would it be?

4. Who should direct the next Star Wars movie?

5. Which movie would you make a sequel to?

6. Which book / comic would you make into an HBO series?

7. How would you end the major conflicts in the world?

8. Which unsung heroes would you elevate to superstardom?

9. Can you believe that the Queen still knights people in the UK. Who would you knight?

IF I RULED THE WORLD...

1. Where would you live?

2. What kind of parties would you throw?

3. Who would be invited?

4. How would you reform politics in your country?

5. If you were in charge of this years Glastonbury/Coachella festivals who would you choose to headline?

6. Who would headline the acoustic stage?

7. If you could watch one band from history play an acoustic set in your front room who would it be?

8. If you could create your own supergroup using any musicians from history who would be the:

    Lead Singer:
    Drummer:
    Bass Guitarist:
    Lead Guitarist:

9. What would the band be called?

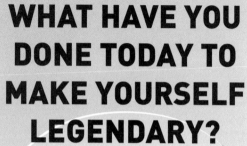

WHAT HAVE YOU DONE TODAY TO MAKE YOURSELF LEGENDARY?

IF YOU WERE A ?, WHICH ? WOULD YOU BE?

'It's not what you're like, it's what you like.'

1. Which music video would you be?

2. Which book would you be?

3. What movie would you be?

4. Which famous person would you be?

5. Which designer label would you be?

6. Which band would you be?

7. Which album would you be?

8. Which song would you be?

9. Which artist would you be?

10. Which comic book would you be?

11. Which TV series would you be?

12. Which team would you be?

13. Which athlete would you be?

14. Which politician would you be?

15. Which musical instrument would you be?

16. Which dance would you be?

SNAPPY CHAT #5

> Find somebody that you know who you would describe as 'introverted' or 'shy' and get them to answer all the questions. Be nice about it. No chinese burns.

2 minutes. 13 questions.

3....2....1....GO!

What's the best thing that's happened to you this week?

What song would be the soundtrack to your life?

What would you call your autobiography?

On a scale of 1 to 10 how excited are you about life right now?

What's the last book that you read?

Which book do you plan on reading next?

Who's your favourite actor?

If you could be a genius of one musical instrument what would it be?

Which book that you read in school had the biggest impact on you?

If they made a movie of your life what would be the song in the opening titles?

What would be the song in the closings credits?

Who would you want to play you in the lead role?

If you could get on a plane and fly to any country in the world right now, where would you choose to go?

LET'S GET PHYSICAL!

We are more than just brains on a stick. Life is a dance.

1. What is your sport and why do you love it?

2. What is your threshold for pain on a scale of 1 to 10?

3. Is it worse to be too hot or too cold?

4. Do you have good or bad circulation?

5. Is your metabolism fast or slow?

6. Where is your home? Your real home? Your sanctuary?

7. How much of your brainspace is occupied by money worries?

8. The struggle is real. Do you ever feel like you might not make it through?

9. Could you run a marathon?

10. Are you an Ectomorph, Endomorph or Mesomorph?

11. If you absolutely had to enter for an Olympic sport which one would it be?

12. Could you swim a mile?

13. Who taught you to ride a bike?

The street is your theatre.
Your life is your masterpiece.

Recognise when the way is open
and when the way is closed.

Learn to read
the patterns in change.

Know when to hold
and when to fold.

When you go deep enough inside,
you find the whole world.

When you go far enough into the
world, you find what is deep inside.

Who asks and who knows?

Hide and seek.
Presence and absence.
Questions and answers.

Repeat forever.

EITHER / OR

You know the drill, one side or t'other.

Lover or Fighter

More Time or More Money

Brains or Beauty

LA or NY

Paris or London

Tokyo or Shanghai

Lisbon or Barcelona

Berlin or Bucharest

Nashville or Memphis

Rational or Emotional

City or Country

Sci-Fi or Action Movie

Thriller or Rom Com

Mountains or Beach

Chess or Checkers

Death Penalty or Life Imprisonment

Good News First or Bad News First

Mayonnaise or Ketchup

Smart or Casual

100k Now or 10k a Year for Life

Attention is our magic power. Focus is our book of spells. Watch how people blossom when you lavish your curiosity upon them. Ask the questions and listen to the answers, it's a really powerful gift to give to anyone. It even works when you give it to yourself.

Studies show that flattery works even when we know it isn't honest. Questions are flattery elevated to an art. Every question here has a secret subtext – and the subtext is always loud and clear . . . you are inherently interesting . . . you are valuable. People believe what you tell them, especially when you hide your messages behind questions.

And why not tell everybody in the world that they are fascinating? It can only make your life more fascinating. If all the people in your world are vindicated by your curiosity about them they will do magical things. Buoyed by the knowledge that their perspective is relevant, they will develop their perspective.

Or more simply put – asking questions is a way of being nice to people. Being nice to people makes life more fun.

THE CLOSEST THING TO CRAZY

We all think we want to fall in love. We fall in love with the idea of falling in love. Then we actually do fall in love and it is very similar to being drugged. All your decisions are made by some kind of star struck, punch drunk rube masquerading as you and then you wake up bankrupt with a screaming baby puking on your face. L'amour bitches! I love you baby. xoxox

1. Do you believe in eternal love?

2. Do you believe in love at first sight?

3. Is there anything about you that others would say is 'quirky'?

4. Can a little insanity be a positive thing?

5. Are you drinking enough water?

6. Are you living for love?

7. If you stripped away all the layers of other people's expectations and desires for you – what would you want for yourself?

8. Are you afraid of making mistakes?

9. What if you could control your fears? How would your life be different?

10. What is the one thing that you are most avoiding doing?

SNAPPY CHAT #6

Also ask these questions to somebody who has authority in your life. Choose a boss, parent, priest, doctor or teacher. Maybe a cop. Be polite!

2 minutes. 17 questions.

3....2....1....GO!

What's the best thing that's happened to you this year?

What's your favourite food?

What's your favourite swear word?

What's your least favourite food?

What do you think is lame right now?

What's your favourite vegetable?

Wash the dishes or dry the dishes?

What's your favourite fruit?

Who was the last person you texted?

What's your favourite drink?

What's your favourite dessert?

Which current band are destined for the Rock and Roll Hall of Fame?

What's your favourite musical genre of all time?

What's your least favourite musical genre of all time?

Who makes you laugh?

Are you any good at maths?

Who do you call when you're bored?

THANK YOU EVERYTHING

Do you ever feel overwhelmed with gratitude? Me neither lol. Jokes. I do. It does happen. Isn't it the best? Would be nice if we could feel that way more often. Not just pretend to feel it in some pious hippy kind of way, but actually feel it. Feel it in that transformative, tears in the eyes kind of way. Anyway. Let's make popcorn!

1. What do you cherish?

2. What are you most grateful for?

3. What made you happy today?

4. If money didn't exist, what work would you choose to do?

5. What do you have to lose?

6. Can you tell the difference between useful criticism and personal attack?

7. What do you think about when you're on your own?

8. What things do you do when you're home alone for hours and you're bored?

9. Who taught you to swim?

MAKE
OTHER PEOPLE
FEEL GOOD
ABOUT
THEMSELVES.

ASK THEM
A QUESTION.

TELL ME A STORY

Fame is largely a question of making your own life into a story for the world to read.

1. Tell me a story about your first kiss.

2. Tell me a story about a fight.

3. Tell me a story about a fantastic day out.

4. Tell me a story about the best night ever.

5. Tell me a story about your school life.

6. Tell me all about that summer after senior school ended...

7. Tell me a story about overcoming.

8. Tell me a sad story.

9. Tell me a funny story.

10. Tell me a story about your friends.

11. Tell me a story about your parents.

12. Tell me a story about screwing up.

13. Tell me a story about an epic win.

14. Tell me a story about when you witnessed karma at work.

15. Tell me your life story in 5 objects.

RUN BABY RUN!

Sometimes I wonder what freedom really means. Because I think maybe we have that messed up in our culture you know? Is it freedom to roll across the earth like a tumbleweed, a rootless thing? But it is in us. That desire to hit the road forever and ever. See the seven seas. Every day a new horizon. Why can't we see what we have with fresh eyes every day?

1. If you started running right now how far could you go without stopping?

2. Do you seek thrills and adrenaline or calm and relaxation?

3. Would you ever eat insects?

4. Should we always prioritise the welfare of humans above that of animals?

5. What is the cause of the obesity epidemic?

6. What are your addictions?

7. Do you/would you give blood?

8. Are you/would you be an organ donor?

9. What tips would you give to someone who was going to take over your body?

10. What is your definition of a beautiful death?

11. If money did not exist and everyone had to barter their services what would you have to offer?

HIGH DEFINITION

Never let go of your right to define the world in your own terms.

Take control. Define your life. Define yourself.

Keep 'em short, sweet and punchy.

Success is...

Love is...

Friendship is...

Happiness is...

Rich is...

Soul is...

Pain is...

Death is...

Funny is...

War is...

Strong is...

Intelligence is...

Creativity is...

SNAPPY CHAT #7

Why not celebrate the fact that you've made it this far by singing all the answers to these questions in the style of an 80's power ballad?

2 minutes. 16 questions.

3....2....1....GO!

What's the best piece of advice that you've been given?

Name your 5 desert island discs?

If you could do a cameo in any movie what would it be?

3 things that make you happy to be alive?

Who's your favourite actress?

Have you ever taken anything from a hotel? (Even soap counts)

What is your favourite word?

What was the last film you saw at the cinema?

When was the last time you danced?

When was the last time that you were scared?

Could you live without your phone for a week?

You have to give up one of your senses for the rest of your life, which one do you choose?

Which sense would you never want to lose?

What's your favourite car of all time?

  – for day to day driving?

  – for posing?

What's your favourite animal?

X OR Y

Maths or English?

Beach Holiday or City Break?

Action or Relaxation?

Lover or Fighter?

Tea or Coffee?

Butter or Spread?

Meat or Vegetables?

Cars or Bicycles?

Planes or Trains?

Cash or Cards?

Poker or Chess?

Kanye or Beyonce?

Football or Soccer?

Church or Nightclub?

Swimming or Cake?

Colouring Books or Sketch Books?

Liberal Arts or Hard Sciences?

Being in Love or Loving for Fun?

Horror Movie or Costume Drama

Loafing or Striving?

Discipline or Spontaneity?

Lyrics or Poetry?

WOULD YOU CHEAT IF YOU KNEW THAT YOU WOULD NEVER BE CAUGHT?

#REALTALK

Is there anything more interesting than talking about other people's lives (other than talking about your own that is)?

1. If you were on death row, what would you choose as your last meal?

2. How many children do you want?

3. How many children should people have?

4. What would you do if you won ten million on the lottery?

5. What would you most like to study?

6. What is your favourite body part in yourself?

7. What is your favourite body part in others?

8. Have you ever had a sudden realisation?

9. Have you ever had your mind completely blown?

10. Who or what motivates you?

11. What have you learnt from your parents?

12. Who is watching out for you?

13. Would you consider cosmetic surgery?

14. What phrase makes no sense to you at all?

SNAPPY CHAT #8

Try this: Answer some questions truthfully and some with outlandish lies. Be careful not to slip into a whirlpool of delusions.

2 minutes. 15 questions.
3....2....1....GO!

What is one thing most people don't know about you?

Which pet do you miss the most?

Do you ever look back?

Are you a daydreamer?

How do you see your future?

Which of your friends do you have the least in common with?

What do you worry about most often?

Do you know your next door neighbours?

How do you calm your mind?

What was the most epic party you went to?

Do you ever question your own ideas?

Do you like exams?

Do you take the trash out?

Do you doubt your own beliefs?

What movie have you watched too many times?

MIND EQUALS BLOWN

WOAH. Like. WOAH.

Questions to drop at 4:00am when everybody has gone quiet.

1. Do you think we'll ever crack time travel?

2. What do you think about evolution?

3. Do you think computers will ever reproduce human intelligence to the extent that we can no longer tell them apart from us?

4. What happens when we die?

5. If the universe is infinitely large then are there an infinite number of worlds exactly the same as this one, with an infinite number of doubles of us experiencing exactly the same things at exactly the same time?

6. What is beauty?

7. What is time?

8. What things do you think will still exist 1,000 years from now?

9. Should we live for today, or tomorrow?

10. Is the world inside your head or outside of your head?

You want
an exciting life?

Ask more
questions.

WOULD YOU RATHER?

Either or neither? You have to choose one. Or do you? Yes. Yes you do.

1. Would you rather be a great singer or a great dancer?

2. Would you rather be a great lover or a great fighter?

3. Would you rather be successful or have really successful children?

4. Would you rather be weird looking and confident or normal looking and shy?

5. Would you rather be really attractive or really funny?

6. Would you rather be very strong or very smart?

7. Would you rather have lots of lovers or one epic love story?

8. Would you rather be 3 inches taller or 3 inches shorter?

9. Would you rather have a life full of highs and lows or one of relative stability.

10. Would you rather live for yourself or live for others?

11. Would you rather dance with the devil or sleep with angels?

WHAT'S THE BEST PIECE OF ADVICE YOU'VE EVER BEEN GIVEN?

WHICH WHICH IS WHICH?

'Which?' asks you to identify something from a closed group of things. It is far more discerning than 'What?'.

1. Which is your planet?

2. Which is your zodiac sign and is it accurate?

3. Which is your poem?

4. Which is your flower?

5. Which is your colour?

6. Which is your number?

7. Which is your day?

8. Which is your month?

9. Which is your year?

10. Which is your smell?

11. Which is your item of clothing?

12. Which is your song?

13. Which is your talisman?

14. Which is your team?

SNAPPY CHAT #9

Here's a little fun twist you could try. Get your buddy to ask you the questions and try to answer every question with a relevant and full counter question. It'll either make you sound like a profound genius or it'll be the most irritating experience ever.

2 minutes. 17 questions.

3....2....1....GO!

How old do you feel inside?

What makes you giggle these days?

Do you make enough time for yourself?

What do you lust for?

Are you scared of anyone in your life?

Can you handle criticism?

What criticism cuts the deepest?

When did you last stay up till sunrise?

How do you use your spare time?

What are your three favourite sounds?

Who are you most alike in your family?

What gives you life?

What made you fall in love?

What do you do that your parents never did?

Describe your favourite scent.

Do you follow your head or your heart?

What comes to mind when you think of summer?

HOW MUCH DO YOU REALLY KNOW ABOUT YOURSELF?

How much can you really know about yourself if you've never survived a zombie apocalypse?

1. What do you miss most about being a child?

2. How long would you survive a zombie apocalypse?

3. Have you ever stolen something?

4. If you could give everybody in the world a thing, (the same thing) what would it be?

5. Your most intense dream ever.

6. Do you believe any conspiracy theories?

7. What is the ideal age to die?

8. What will be on the playlist at your funeral party?

9. Do you consider yourself an adult?

10. Are you what you say, what you do or what you are?

11. To what extent do you make your own fate?

12. What is the one thing that you are most passionate about?

GET OFF
THE FENCE!

You are King Solomon for a day. The world needs your justice. Get out those weighing scales and polish up that sword. And put on your blindfold because justice is blind.

Now get down off that fence before you fall off!

Feminism
The Job is Done or The Struggle Continues?

Crime
Social Problem or Personal Responsibility?

Cloning
Scientific Advancement or Ethically Wrong?

Nuclear Power
Clean and Green or Accident Waiting to Happen?

Boycott Israel
Anti-Semitic Conspiracy or Legitimate Protest?

Wikileaks
Truth Campaigner or Loose Cannon?

Censorship
Nanny State Meddling
or Essential to Protect the Innocent?

GET OFF
THE FENCE!

Tech giants
Visionary Innovators or Tax Shy Profit Diverters?

Smacking Kids
Useful Parenting Tool or Abuse of Power?

The Kardashians
Pointless Celebrities or Superstar Role Models?

Modern Art
Massive Con or Culturally Important?

Abortion
Should be Freely Available or Heavily Restricted?

Advertising
Corporate Mind Control or Innocent Selling Tool?

Driverless Cars
The Future of Travel
or A Road to Nowhere and Bound to End in Tears?

ADHD
Mental Health Problem or Medical Fashion?

Space Exploration
Mans Final Frontier or Frivolous Waste of Money?

THE RIGHT QUESTION AT THE RIGHT TIME CAN OPEN THE DOORS TO HIDDEN WORLDS.

DON'T TALK ABOUT POLITICS AND RELIGION!

If you want everybody to love you, you have to make 'em all think that you're on their side.

1. Is it easier for rich kids to be successful?

2. What is your earliest memory?

3. What would you like to be named after you?

4. Do you ever fantasise about having a farm?

5. What does God look like?

6. If you could save one endangered species which would you choose?

7. Describe your dream holiday, fantasy style, no restrictions.

8. What was the best holiday you ever had in real life?

9. If you could save a thousand innocents by killing one innocent, would you?

10. What's the biggest change you've made in your life?

11. Do you ever tell lies?

12. Is it OK for really poor people to steal?

SNAPPY CHAT #10

> When you have done these questions, take the last human being who phoned you and send them your favourite three questions from the list. Why not? C'mon! It'll be fun I promise. You can blame the book if it all goes wrong.

2 minutes. 16 questions.

3....2....1....GO!

You can spend a day of leisure with anyone, who do you choose?

Do you have two way conversations in your own head?

When was the last time you cried in public?

Do you make New Years' Resolutions?

Do you ever rehearse situations?

Do you look good in photographs?

What have you overplayed recently?

How do you deal with waiting for something?

Do you leave the party first, last or in between?

Do you have matching kitchenware?

What's the best movie to watch with children?

Who would you like to know better than you do?

What makes you different to everybody else?

Can you roll with the punches?

Do you ever dance alone?

Would you rather be older than you are or younger than you are?

ONE WORD

There is a sublime freedom in limitation.

You have only one word to say everything you have to say about the following topics. One word for each. No cheating.

There is a sublime truth in spontaneity.

Take the first word that comes into your head. Don't think. Do it fast. Really fast.

Ready...?

Life	Magic
Celebrity	Greed
Religion	Happiness
Love	Evil
Success	Poverty
Future	Earth
Past	Home
Present	Sex
Power	Truth
Politics	Progress
Community	Hope
Death	Inspiration

PEOPLE BELIEVE YOU ARE WHAT YOU SAY YOU ARE

SO, WHAT DO YOU KNOW?

You have gone back in time to the year 1500. After a series of incredible adventures you have been taken into the care of Renaissance genius Leonardo da Vinci. He teaches you to speak Italian in a matter of months. Now he is plying you with questions about the future...

Can you explain to Leonardo these basic facts of contemporary life in the 21st century:

1. So what is this Big Bang idea?

2. How do you harness electricity?

3. How do you make a lightbulb?

4. How do you vaccinate against diseases?

5. How do you make penicillin?

6. What is a computer and what does it do?

7. What is the internet?

8. How do you make a car?

9. What can you tell me about atoms?

10. What are the laws of physics?

11. What actually happened in the Hunger Games?

12. What is dark matter?

13. Who rules the world?

14. How do you fight wars?

WHO ARE YOU AND WHAT DO YOU WANT TO SAY TO THE WORLD?

I HAVE MEASURED OUT MY LIFE WITH...

...Coffee spoons / Phone Games / Knitting / Crack Pipes / Cable TV (Delete as appropriate).

1. How many hours a week do you watch TV?

2. How many hours a week do you spend online?

3. How many hours a week do you spend playing sports?

4. If you took 50% of those hours and use them to create stuff, how many hours a week would you be creating stuff? How many songs could you write, videos could you post, articles, poems, blog posts etc?

5. Do you celebrate your victories?

6. Do you celebrate your friends' victories?

7. If you could learn a skill or acquire a talent immediately what would you choose?

8. You have twenty hours to invest in acquiring a new skill. How will you spend them?

9. As a member of the tiny percentage of humans in history that have been educated to be able to read and write and to have been blessed with the miracle of leisure time and the presence of some degree of disposable income in your life – how lucky do you feel on a scale of one to ten?

10. How many languages do you speak?

SNAPPY CHAT #11

Why not try to flip the script once in a while. Shout out an answer and make your friends guess the question. Funniest guess wins.

2 minutes. 17 questions.
3....2....1....GO!

What is your vocation?

Have you ever been in love with a famous person?

What song always makes you happy?

When did you last feel acutely embarrassed?

What's your achilles heel?

What did you not know you'd got till it had gone?

Which country do you want to visit next?

What past event would you like to have witnessed?

Have you ever Googled your own name?

What is your signature dinner party dish?

Which is your favourite shop in the world?

Who is the most famous person you have met?

How many books do you read in the average year?

Are the best things in life free?

What is your favourite way to get from a to b?

Do you usually speak your mind?

What would you most like to be famous for?

TO BE
OR NOT TO BE

How often do we truly make irreversible decisions of great consequence? Should we go with the flow or try to impose our will upon our life situations? Do we ever really know what we want? To be or not to be?

1. What is the difference between life and survival?

2. Do you ask enough questions?

3. Would you ever adopt a child?

4. Would you ever do a parachute jump?

5. Someone hands you a telephone and tells you to talk to God. What do you ask her?

6. If you could swap lives with somebody else for a week, who would you choose and why? How would you brief them for a week of being you?

7. You can travel to the future or the past. Which time period would you choose and why?

8. Would you donate your body to medical science?

9. Queue jumping - acceptable or abhorrent?

ARE WE HAVING FUN YET?

Come inside the sanctuary of your mind and take a look around. Take a question in your hand like a flashlight and shine it around the old place. Here and there you see the piled up boxes of your life experience. Here is where you find the building blocks of you. You don't get to choose exactly what you find in here – but you do get to choose how you put it all together, reconstructing the pieces in new ways to play new games. Like a box of Lego. Like a dressing up box. Doesn't it make life more fun when you realise that identity is a game?

It's not a joke. It's a game. Big difference. It can be funny. It can hurt too. And like all the best games – it can be a crisis – an identity crisis.

Definition:
When you get stuck in a definition that no longer fits.

Then there is the old story of the phoenix – the bird that burns itself alive to emerge reborn from the ashes. That's a helluva price to pay for reinventing yourself.

Then, that's the difference between recreating yourself and just pretending to be something you're not – risk.

Go all in.

ARE WE HAVING FUN YET?

ARE YOU TALKING TO ME?

Nobody ever got famous by keeping their mouth shut. Answer the following question out loud: Do you ever talk to yourself?

1. Do you talk to your plants?
2. Do you talk to your pets?
3. Do you talk to your things?
4. Do you talk to your TV?
5. Do you talk to strangers?
6. Do you talk to people enough?
7. Do you talk to old people?
8. Do you talk to children?
9. Do you talk to any of your body parts?
10. Do you #realtalk?
11. Do you #smalltalk?
12. Do you have a catchphrase?
13. Do you, like, say, like, any particular words, like, too much, y'know like?
14. Do you talk too much or too little or just enough?
15. Do you listen to people or think about what you're going to say when they finish talking?
16. Do you judge a book by its cover?
17. Are you good at talking people into things?
18. Are you good at talking people out of things?

IF I RULED
THE WORLD...

We spend most of our lives lusting after a little bit more power, what if we actually got all the power we ever wanted and a truckload more? What would you really do with it if you had it?

1. If you could get any two artists in history to collaborate on a piece of art who would you choose?

2. If you could referee two celebrities having a mixed martial arts fight who would you choose?

3. Who would win?

4. If you could get any two singers in history (living or dead) into the studio to record a duet who would you choose?

5. What song would they sing?

7. Who would you throw in jail?

8. If you could get your all time favourite band to record a cover song, what would you want it to be?

9. How would you punish the guys who put all the adverts on YouTube?

IF I RULED
THE WORLD...

1. How corrupt would you be on scale of one to ten?

2. What would you ban?

3. How would you treat your enemies?

4. What would you get rid of?

5. What websites would you shut down?

6. What projects would you fund?

7. What wonders would you build to commemorate your glorious reign?

8. What would you do with the Olympics?

9. Who would you put in charge to carry out your commands?

10. What kind of spectacles would you put on to win the loyalty of your people?

11. Who would you throw into prison without trial?

SNAPPY CHAT #12

> Download the Google Translate app. That thing is pure witchcraft. You just point your phone camera at the text and it translates it right in front of your eyes. Now translate the questions into Spanish and go and find a Spanish speaker to ask. Revel in your awful pronunciation.

2 minutes. 14 questions.
3....2....1....GO!

Name three apps you use every week..

What is your most useless talent?

Which superstar would you most like to go on vacation with?

Would your childhood self be proud of who you have become?

Have you ever been really let down by a person you trusted?

What is your most glorious epic win of all time?

Which bit of housework do you like the most?

What's your favourite month?

Who knows you the best?

What is the first thing you think about when you wake up?

Are you OK with admitting you were wrong?

Do you hold grudges?

Are you a good loser?

Would you rather be the one answering the questions or asking the questions?

THIRTEEN WHO'S (AND NO HORTON)

Who is the wisest of the wh- question words - this is because owls say it. Whoo Whoo.

1. Who is your character reference?

2. Who is your best friend?

3. Who is your bodyguard?

4. Who is your attorney?

5. Who is your stunt double?

6. Who is your accountant?

7. Who is your guardian angel?

8. Who is your partner-in-crime?

9. Who will you be reincarnated as in your next life?

10. Who were you in your past lives?

11. Who is your soulmate?

12. Who is the one that got away?

13. Who has been the most influential person in your life to date?

REFLECTIONS

It's nice to have a role. It's nice to be 'that guy' or 'that girl'. But roles are, by definition, limiting. Sometimes that is a good thing. Sometimes it is not. Roles are your reflection in the eyes of others.

Narcissus fell in love with his reflection. When you fall in love with your image, you cannot change. Not changing is not living. Not living is being dead – or rather 'dead in life' which is to say – undead. Like a zombie. Like a sixty year old superstar addicted to cosmetic surgery.

The image that we cast on pools of water, (narcissus), in mirrors (wicked witch), in shop windows (everybody else) – it's only a fragment pretending to be whole, pretending to be the whole of reality.

Questions make far better mirrors.

The reflection in your head is the one that counts. But it needs to be constantly updated. Questions are the best medicine.

Can you learn to love and let go?

Be kind to yourself and self critical?

Know yourself without self-obsession?

Reflect on your actions without overthinking?

Can you ever really see your true reflection? Or, fairy like, does it disappear when you look directly at it?

LITTLE RITUALS

You know, like making a cup of tea, setting the table for guests or organising a Black Mass.

1. If you had ten minutes on national TV, what would you talk to the nation about?

2. What is under your bed right now?

3. If you could go to the refrigerator right now and find one thing, what would you want it to be?

4. What is in your refrigerator right now?

5. How many hats do you own?

6. How many shoes do you own?

7. What % of your clothes do you wear less than once a month?

8. Which side of the bed do you sleep on?

9. Do you have any little rituals?

10. Are you a little bit OCD?

11. Pet hates?

12. What colour is your underwear right now?

13. What are you allergic to?

14. What nationality do you not care for?

15. Whats the best thing to put on toast?

WOULD YOU PASS
A LIE DETECTOR
TEST?

RATE YOURSELF

It is somewhat perverse how much we as a species enjoy measuring ourselves.

1. Rate your memory from 1-10

2. Rate your sex appeal from 1-10

3. Rate your chat from 1-10

4. Rate your sense of humour from 1-10

5. Rate your style from 1-10

6. Rate your game from 1-10

7. Rate your fitness from 1-10

8. Rate your diet from 1-10

9. Rate your intelligence from 1-10

10. Rate your emotional intelligence from 1-10

11. Rate your social skills from 1-10

12. Rate you 'fun to be with' ness 1-10

13. Rate your sporting prowess 1-10

14. Rate your fighting skills 1-10

15. Rate your dancing 1-10

SNAPPY CHAT #13

> Eyes down, look in, it's time for some more snappy chat...

2 minutes. 19 questions.
3....2....1....GO!

What colours do you wear most often?

What do you thank your parents for?

Do you believe that your horoscope is accurate?

Do you put your work before your loves?

Have you ever broken the law?

What do you like to do on a night out?

What should you really give more time to?

Do you like being the centre of attention?

Are you a good driver?

What word or phrase do you overuse?

If you never needed money, what would you do for work?

Do you enjoy a bit of solitude?

Do you say yes more often than you say no?

What unusual things make you happy?

Do you have any loose ends to tie up?

Have you seen a UFO?

What makes you cry?

What makes you sneeze?

What makes you stay up late?

PERFECT
AS YOUR ARE

Outside the sacred game of hide and seek sits your perfect self, unaffected by the winning and the losing.

1. What is the most important lesson you have learned?

2. What is your favourite food?

3. Favourite smell?

4. Favourite sound?

5. Favourite thing to eat on the sofa while watching movies?

6. Worst feeling in the world?

7. Best feeling in the world?

8. What is your home screen image on your phone?

9. Describe your profile picture.

10. Do you still have any soft toys?

11. Do you enjoy thunderstorms?

12. What is your favourite snack?

13. Do you eat your greens?

ONE LOVE

Call them like you see them.

**You pays your money and you takes your choice
(you can choose only one)**

Starter, Main Course or Dessert

MP3, CD, Vinyl or Tape

Beach, City Break, Adventure, Skiing, or Cruise

Window, Middle or Aisle

Cat, Dog, Rabbit, Goldfish or Canary

Late Nights or Early Mornings

John, Paul, Ringo or George

Tokyo, NY, London, Rome, Barcelona, LA or Paris

Spring, Summer, Autumn or Winter

Jazz, Classical, Blues, Reggae or R&B

De Niro, Cruise, Nicholson, Di Caprio,
Hanks or Brando

Internet, TV, Gaming, Music or Sport

Rare, Medium Rare, Medium or Well Done

ONE LOVE

Boiled, Scrambled, Sunny Side Up or Over Easy

Star Wars I, II, III, IV, V, VI or VII

Sunrise or Sunset

Stephen King, Tolkien, Dickens, J.K. Rowling,
Orwell or Roald Dahl

Abstract, Pop Art, Street Art, Surrealism
or Contemporary

Prius, Porsche, Mini, Ferrari or Range Rover

Good News First or Bad News First

Hitchcock, Kubrick, Spielberg, Scorsese or Tarantino

The Godfather, Gone With The Wind, Star Wars,
Frozen or Forrest Gump

Art, Music, Crafts, Gaming or Reading

Hip Hop, Rock, Pop, Heavy Metal,
Country or Dance

Hepburn, Streep, Bullock, Lawrence or Monroe

Museum, Gallery, Gig or Theme Park

The Beginning or The End

SNAPPY CHAT #14

> Now ask these questions to the person that you care for the most.

2 minutes. 20 questions.
3....2....1....GO!

Who was the last person you spoke to?

Where is home?

What is home?

What song makes you get on the dance floor?

What word makes you cringe?

How many real friends do you have right now?

Do you ever meditate?

Do you give people a second chance?

Who is your oldest friend?

Who is your oddest friend?

What was the most money you ever spent on a thing?

Do you know where the boundaries are?

What do you most appreciate in a loved one?

Do you have a hero who fell from grace?

Are you a patient person?

How do you feel about kids?

What is your favourite colour?

Describe your hairstyle in one word.

What's your favourite mythical animal?

What is your default: Pessimism or Optimism?

EITHER / OR

Facebook or Twitter

The Book or The Movie

Early Bird or Night Owl

Board Games or Video Games

Cats or Dogs

Super Hero or Super Villain

Pepsi or Coke

Money or Fame

Waffles or Pancakes

Sunrise or Sunset

Head or Heart

Pension or Property

Fiction or Non Fiction

Call or Text

Piercings or Tattoos

Stage or Screen

Mac or PC

Introvert or Extrovert

Reincarnation or Nothing

Pizza or Pasta

Sand or Snow

Fast Food or Fresh Food

When your fascination for others is infinite you become infinitely more fascinating.

HIGH SCHOOL DAZE

You spend half your youth at school then you spend half your adult life recovering from school.

1. Who was your worst teacher?

2. Who was the class clown?

3. Who was the dumbest person at school?

4. Who was the 'biggest pain in the ass'?

6. Did you enjoy being at high school?

7. What kind of student were you at high school?

8. What are your best memories of high-school?

9. What are your worst memories of high school?

10. Who was your favourite teacher and why?

11. Who do you wish a horrible revenge upon?

12. Who do wish great success upon?

DIGGING DEEPER STILL

Here we go again, its time to go even deeper.

1. Is it Ok to be slightly economical with the truth when you're filling in your tax return?

2. Should animals be used for cosmetic testing?

3. Should animals be used for scientific/health testing?

4. If you were a world class athlete and you knew that some competitors were using banned substances would you take them in order to compete?

5. Would you take banned substances if you knew 100% of the competition were taking them?

6. If you knew your friends' partner was being unfaithful, would you tell them?

7. You buy a new shirt and after wearing it once you decide that you don't like it. Is it OK to return it?

8. If reincarnation was real, what do you think you would come back as?

9. The cashier at the supermarket has given you too much change. Do you tell them?

X OR Y

Tragedy or Comedy?

Ducks or Geese?

TV or Radio?

Girls or Boys?

Colourful or Monochrome?

Apples or Pears?

Penguins or Ostriches?

Rock or Rap?

Punk or Disco?

Water or Wine?

East Coast or West Coast?

German or French?

Wolves or Dragons?

Fabulous or Awesome?

Refined or Primal?

Pulled Pork or Beef Brisket?

Deep & Smokey or Fresh & Aromatic?

Cautious or Carefree?

Heavy Metal or Banging Techno?

Hi-Fi Separates or Bluetooth Speaker?

SNAPPY CHAT #15

Answer this next set of questions in a French accent.

2 minutes. 18 questions.

3....2....1....GO!

What song makes you run away from the dancefloor?

What is on your bedside table?

What has been the biggest pain in the ass?

Who are you angry with at the moment?

What or who did you last discover?

When did you last feel the fear and do it anyway?

How well do you sleep?

Are you a memorable person?

What is your relationship with physical exercise?

Do you judge gently or can you be quite harsh?

Why are you doing the work you are doing now?

What hobby would you like more time for?

Who should everyone be listening to right now?

If you could have a walk on part in any TV series (past or present) what would it be?

What is your favourite thing in life right now?

What is your favourite Hitchcock Movie?

What is your favourite Spielberg Movie?

What is your favourite movie of all time?

KEYBOARD WARRIOR

I can't come to bed yet honey. Somebody is wrong on the internet.

1. Can you recognise a leading question when you see one?

2. Are you good at arguing?

3. Are you largely emotional or largely rational in a debate?

4. Do you think it is ever possible to be truly objective?

5. Do you ever try and see things from somebody else's point of view?

6. Is it important to you that somebody is told when they are completely wrong?

7. Do you turn a blind eye when somebody is completely wrong for the sake of an easy life?

8. Do you call people out for racism, sexism, ignorance or bigotry?

9. Do you think it's OK if it's only joking?

10. Do you enjoy conflict?

11. Do you avoid conflict?

12. Are you in control of your emotions or do they control you?

TELL ME
A SECRET

DANCING IN THE RAIN

I think this whole idea that happiness depends on the weather is overplayed. If you can't crack a smile on a miserable winter's day you won't be much fun in the summer either. In my country we say 'We're not made of paper'. We also eat too many sausage rolls. What have we learned? Get out there and dance in the rain!

1. What was the last competition you entered?
2. What was the last game you played?
3. Do you know any good gossip?
4. Have you ever been arrested?
5. Have you ever danced in the rain?
6. What is your blood type?
7. Have you ever had your fortune told?
8. If you ordered a pizza right now what would it be?
9. Your first thought when you woke up this morning.
10. Should we tell children the whole truth or shelter them from harsh reality?
11. What is the weirdest thing you have eaten?
12. Which Muppet are you?
13. Do you plan your life or live in the moment?

CHASING WATERFALLS

Now that our dreams are colonised only those who don't dream are truly free. #NEVERPLAY

1. If you dropped everything right now and went off to seek your fortune, what would you do and where would you go?

2. If you left everything you have to chase a dream, what would you lose?

3. What makes you special?

4. What do you long for?

5. What do you daydream about?

6. What do you need?

7. What do you do for the people you love?

8. If you had 24 hours to live, what would you do?

9. If you had one year to live, what would you do?

10. What bad habits do you want to lose?

11. Is anyone living rent free in your head?

12. Who or what are the time thieves in your life?

13. Who is taking and not giving?

YOUNG, GIFTED & HUNGRY

The path of the righteous is beset with problems. Follow your heart and you'll often go hungry. But it's worth it in the end. Let the comfortable people play it safe. Choose adventure. Even when it makes you late for dinner. Better to be alive and struggling than rich and bored, right?

1. Describe the next five years of your life in one sentence.

2. Describe the last five years of your life in one sentence.

3. When did you last do something new?

4. What inspires you?

5. What puts a fire under your ass?

6. Who makes you want to be better?

7. What are your core values? Give us three.

8. What do you love to do?

9. How often do you do what you love?

10. What stops you from doing what you love?

11. What can you do today that you could not do this time last year?

SNAPPY CHAT #16

> Now ask the next person you meet these questions.

2 minutes. 19 questions.
3....2....1....GO!

Is your finger on the pulse?

What accessories do you wear every day?

Do you always know when it's time to go home?

Do you ever get scared of the dark?

What's your regular order in a cafe?

Save the money or spend the money?

Name a book that blew your mind.

Losing weight: diet or workout?

The last magazine you read was?

When did you last stroke a cat?

What do you look back on with rose tinted glasses?

Do you have any guilty pleasures?

When did you last hold a baby?

How many places have you lived in?

Would you like a different name?

How does it feel to be heartbroken?

What should you throw away but you just can't let go of?

What is the sexiest accent?

Are you always right?

SHINE
YOUR LIGHT

Hey you! Yeah you! We all need you to shine your light! So take down all those hang-ups and fears that you cover it up with and toss them in the fire. We need you. We all need you. We need ALL of you.

1. What has been your greatest adventure?

2. What are you proud of?

3. What is your greatest strength?

4. What is your most appealing personality trait?

5. How many true friends are enough?

6. Who needs you?

7. If you could make one thing in the world disappear right now, what would it be?

8. Who would miss you most if you left tomorrow?

9. What did you learn today?

10. If the whole world was listening what would you say?

Do you ever do that thing where you imagine you're being interviewed? In your head, your actions and motivations are being gently scrutinised by a sympathetic Oprah / Ellen / Jimmy Fallon while you bare all for the fans. Or is that just me?

You know what I mean. We all do it.

Some people like to imagine what life will be like when they've finally made the big time. We enjoy daydreaming about the big exclusive interview that comes after. The big chance to really tell our side of the story – to a world that is already hanging on our every word.

There's no harm in a little dreaming.

The great thing about this kind of indulgence is that it comes for free. Give yourself permission to give yourself attention. And sometimes that might mean switching your phone off – letting yourself get bored – giving yourself a little space to fill with a daydream.

Let's make sure we don't eradicate daydreaming by filling up every spare moment with an app and a status update.

Waiting for something – just plain old sitting and waiting, can be the most creative thing you do all day.

Oh wait I'm totally going to Twitter that.

YOU MUST CREATE

In my head there is only one commandment. You Must Create. It is the only power we truly own. Making Stuff is Being Human. EVERYBODY IS AN ARTIST. And you do not need an audience to justify creating whatever the hell you want to create. So, I'm just going to keep on crocheting fractals and you do your thing.

1. Have you done anything lately that you'll remember forever?

2. When was the last time you were in a completely new place?

3. What are you excited about?

4. What are you reading?

5. What are you studying?

6. What are you learning to do?

7. What skills are you working on?

8. What ideas are in your ideas book?

9. What have you made recently?

10. Do you ever think about other people's problems?

11. Do you ask enough questions?

GET OFF
THE FENCE!

**Stop. Say what you think. Maybe you're wrong.
Maybe you're not. How you gonna grow if you never
say what you really think? Maybe there are two sides
to every story. Maybe there is a wrong and a right...**

Vote or Don't Vote
Abstention is a Legitimate Form of Protest
or A Foolish Waste of a Hard Won Right?

Is Sport Really News
Sport is Life
or Stupid Ball Games Get Too Much Coverage?

New World Order
They Rule or Conspiracy is for Fools?

Copyright
Information Wants to be Free
or Creators Should Own Their Ideas?

Government Surveillance
Nothing to Hide = Nothing to Fear
or Big Brother is Watching You = Creeping Fascism?

Gambling
Fun Hobby if You Know Your Limits
or Shameless Exploitation of Desperate People?

GET OFF
THE FENCE!

Tipping
Reward for Good Service
or Wage Subsidy for Low Paid?

Politicians
Voice of the People or Self Serving Charlatans?

Vegetables
Organically Grown and Wonky
or Genetically Modified and Perfect?

Fast Food
Convenient, Cheap and Tasty
or Cut Out the Middleman and
Flush it Straight Down the Toilet?

The Royal Family
A National Institution
or Irrelevant, Outmoded and Unelected?

Welfare State
Safety Net for Needy
or Crutch for Work Shy Spongers

Scientology
Wackadoodle Weird UFO Cult
or A Spiritual Path to Enlightenment?

**We're all so terrified
of getting bored.
We won't let a moment pass
without consuming some data.
We won't wait for anything
without some kind of digital
distraction to fill the time.**

**Play a little game with yourself.
Let yourself get bored.**

**Wallow in it.
Don't be afraid of it.
Push it as far as you can.**

**Something always happens.
Some new idea, some fresh
perspective appears.**

Nature abhors a vacuum.

**The spark of inspiration
needs an empty cave.**

X OR Y

Classic or Contemporary?

Apple or Android?

Digital Native or Digital Immigrant?

Hackable or Secure?

Real Camera or Phone Camera?

Instagram or Snapchat?

Live Music or Live Sport?

On Stage or In the Audience?

Indy or Mainstream?

Blogs or Podcasts?

Comic Convention or Gaming Convention?

Twin Peaks or True Detective?

Revolution or Evolution?

Gardening or Soldering?

Brand New or Thrifted?

Making Stuff or Buying Stuff?

Knitting or Sewing?

Adventure or Inner Peace?

Creativity or Knowledge?

Night on the Tiles or Evening by the Fire?

Spirituality or Religion?

Save or Spend?

Autobiography or Graphic Novel

SNAPPY CHAT #17

Now ask your best friend these questions.

2 minutes. 17 questions.
3....2....1....GO!

Which is your favourite room?

What is your (actually achievable) dream?

Do you buy flowers?

What time do you get up in the mornings?

Did you have a happy childhood?

Do you believe in aliens?

How long do you spend in the bath or shower?

When did you last do absolutely nothing all day long?

On a scale of one to ten how well did you do at school?

Which is your season?

Describe your face in three words.

What do you kick yourself for missing?

Are you violently competitive?

The best time of the day is...?

What is your typing speed?

If I gave you ten grand to start a business, what would you do with it?

Do you care what others say?

DIGGING EVEN DEEPER

Yes, it's more deep and meaningful questions...

1. If you were hungry would you steal?

2. What/who would you be prepared to die for?

3. What/who would you be prepared to kill for?

4. Would you lie to someone you loved to protect them?

5. If you won 5 million on the lottery, how much would you give to charity?

6. Your best friend just left their diary behind after visiting you, do you read it?

7. You are given the opportunity to discover the exact date you will die. Would you want to know?

8. Who/what have you got a beef with?

9. Should we always forgive?

10. Is there any hope for us?

11. What is the way forward?

12. What were you put on this Earth to do?

13. Would you cheat in an exam if you knew that you wouldn't be caught?

Alright, OK. So I'm just a big book of questions and you're just a monkey made of stardust that can decipher the reflected light from this page and transform it into an invisible voice in your head that you perceive to be inside your skull, and you perceive to belong to someone else, and you perceive this voice as sound even though there are no such vibrations tickling your cochlea.

What was my point? Well, I guess (incidentally, what does my voice sound like inside your head?) what it comes down to is this.

We all want to escape from the drudgery of everyday life to a realm of infinite possibility. And we call this realm 'fame and fortune' even though, and you can ask them yourself, people who have 'fame and fortune' never escape from everyday life.

Now this is one of those things that we all know, but we pretend not to know because our whole society would fall apart if we all stopped believing that one day we're gonna be superstars / superheroes / maverick billionaires - delete as appropriate.

And maybe that is fine, because this game of foolish desires is as fine a way as any to spend a lifetime, unless of course the cost of the charade is too high, which is another story, but look closely and you'll see in this a hard kernel of hopeful truth which is hopefully true...

And that is simply that everyday life already is miraculous, cosmic, glittering and filled with infinite possibilities. The problem lies only in our perception of it.

If you can learn to clear away the accumulated dust of used-up thoughts from the windowsill of your third eye, then you will experience life - your own life - as an epic legend equal to any story ever told - which, of course, it already is.

And maybe one day, enough people will do the same, and there will be a tipping point, a gentle awakening.

And we can all feel like stars. All the time.

And then we'll probably want something else.

Because we're hopeless.

BYE (FOR NOW)

It's been emotional. We want to thank you for being such a fabulous guest. Your life is an art installation and we were privileged to be a part of that. We wish you all the best.

The amazing thing about human beings is that we never stop growing. One day you like coffee and cigarettes the next day you like frozen yogurt and triathlons. Who knew? Change is our tragedy and our hope. It is also what keeps our relationships with others alive.

So if you've exhausted all the questions here, say goodbye and stick the book under your bed for a year. Then rediscover it while chasing an escaped gerbil and suddenly discover that your answers to half the questions have changed.

You never set foot in the same river twice. And some days an answer is already only half true by the time it falls out of your mouth.

It's only when you think you know everything that you start to get old.

Question everything all the time.

It's exhausting - but it's better this way.

All the answers in the world will never be enough.

Game Over.

Continue?